Russia

by Grace Hansen

Abdo Kids Jumbo is an Imprint of Abdo Kids
abdobooks.com

abdobooks.com

Published by Abdo Kids, a division of ABDO, P.O. Box 398166, Minneapolis, Minnesota 55439.

Printed in China

052019

092019

Photo Credits: Alamy, iStock, Shutterstock

Production Contributors: Teddy Borth, Jennie Forsberg, Grace Hansen
Design Contributors: Dorothy Toth, Pakou Moua

Library of Congress Control Number: 2018963338

Publisher's Cataloging-in-Publication Data

Names: Hansen, Grace, author.

Title: Russia / by Grace Hansen.

Description: Minneapolis, Minnesota : Abdo Kids, 2020 | Series: Countries | Includes online resources and index.

Identifiers: ISBN 9781532185540 (lib. bdg.) | ISBN 9781532186523 (ebook) | ISBN 9781532187018 (Read-to-me ebook)

Subjects: LCSH: Russia--Juvenile literature. | Russia--History--Juvenile literature. | Eurasia--Juvenile literature. | Geography--Juvenile literature.

Classification: DDC 947--dc23

Table of Contents

Russia 4

Major Cities. 12

Plants & Animals 16

The Arts 20

Awesome Landmarks in Russia 22

Glossary 23

Index 24

Abdo Kids Code. 24

Russia

Russia is in Eastern Europe and Northern Asia. It is the largest country in the world by area.

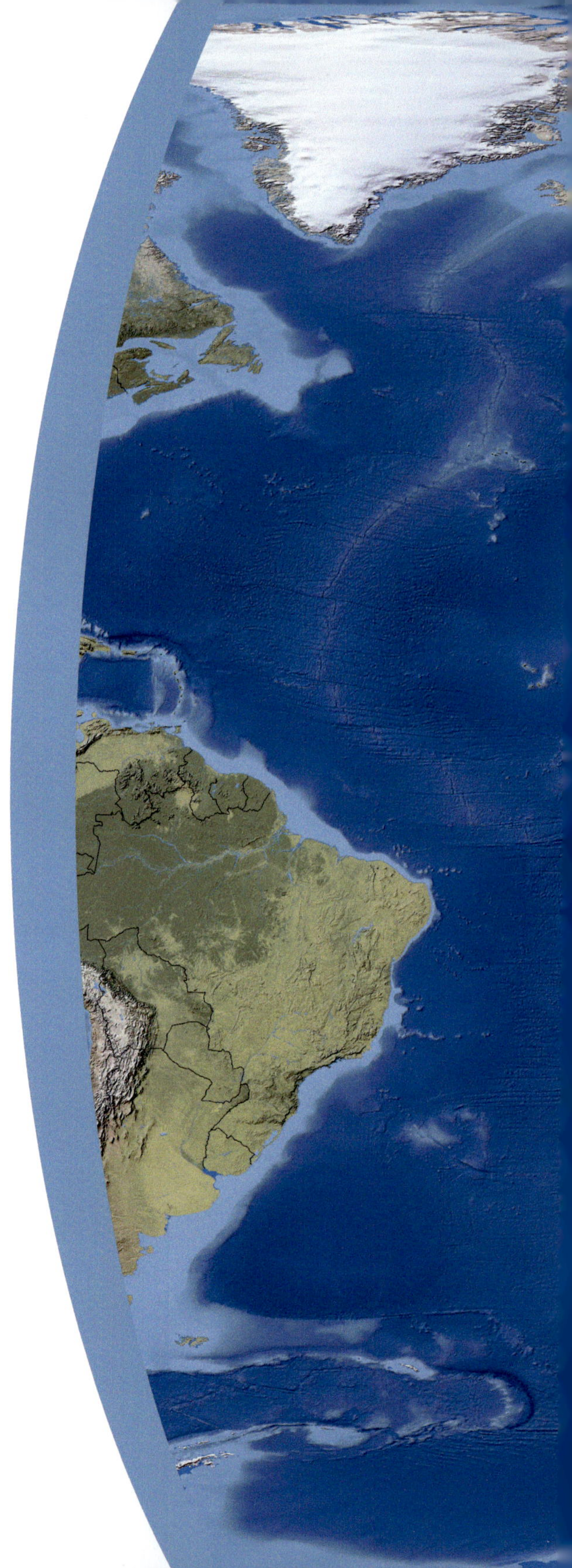

Arctic Ocean
Russia
Europe
Asia
Pacific Ocean
Africa
Australia
N
W
E
S

Because Russia is so huge, it has many climates and **biomes**. It has everything from low plains to soaring mountains. It also has **tundra**, forests, deserts, and beaches.

7

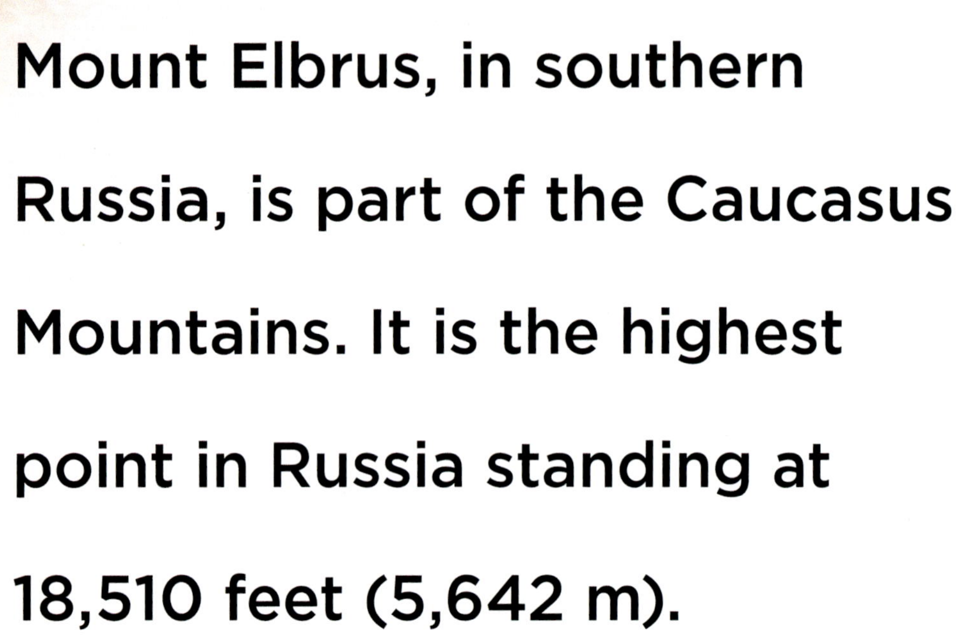

Mount Elbrus, in southern Russia, is part of the Caucasus Mountains. It is the highest point in Russia standing at 18,510 feet (5,642 m).

Russia has nearly 23,000 miles (37,015 km) of **coastline**. The Pacific and Arctic Oceans touch much of the nation.

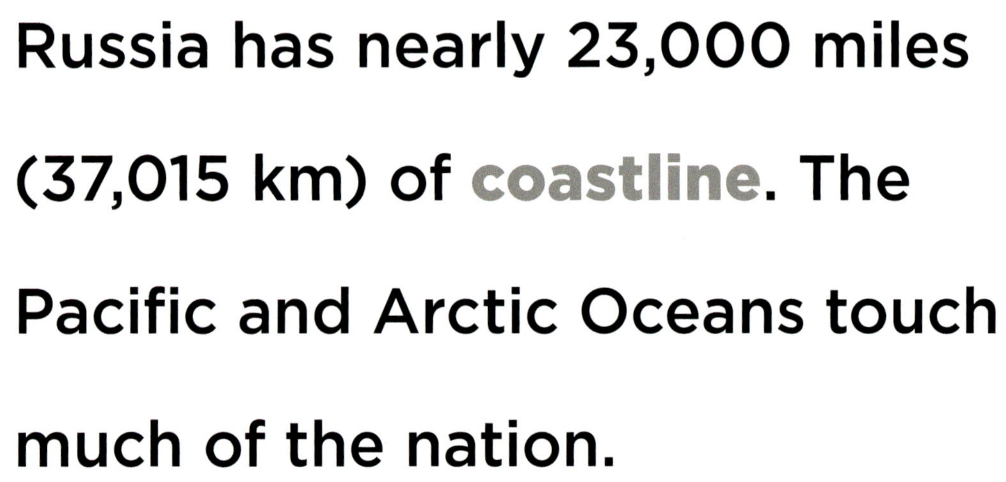

Major Cities

Most of Russia's population lives in the western part of the country. Moscow is Russia's capital. It is one of the largest cities in the world. Nearly 12 million people live there.

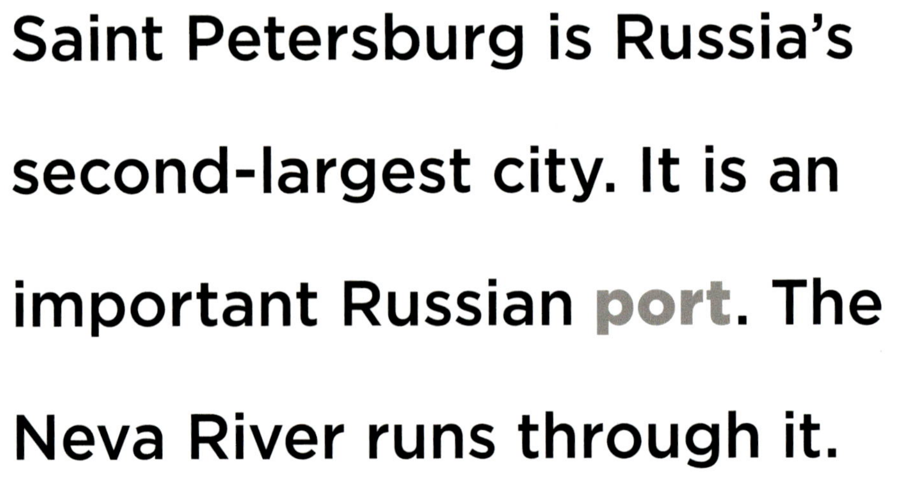

Saint Petersburg is Russia's second-largest city. It is an important Russian **port**. The Neva River runs through it.

Plants & Animals

Russia is filled with amazing plants and animals. Siberian tigers live in far-eastern Russia. They are the largest cats in the world!

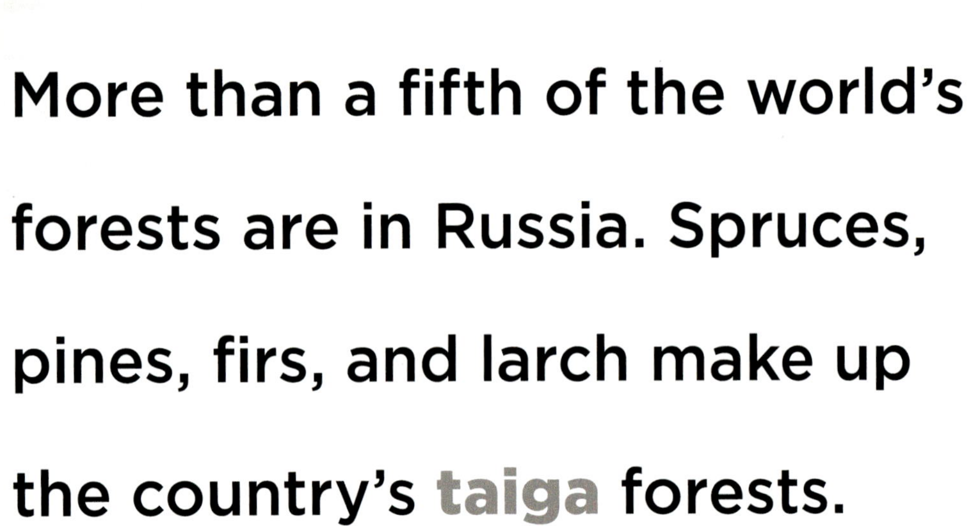

More than a fifth of the world's forests are in Russia. Spruces, pines, firs, and larch make up the country's **taiga** forests.

The Arts

Many famous 18th century writers were Russian. Leo Tolstoy was born in Russia in 1828. He is best known for his novels *War and Peace* and *Anna Karenina*.

ANNA
KARENINA
TOLSTOY
WAR
&
PEACE

Awesome Landmarks in Russia

Ergaki National Park
Krasnoyarsk Krai, Russia

Lake Baskunchak
Astrakhan Oblast, Russia

St. Basil's Cathedral
Moscow, Russia

Winter Palace
Saint Petersburg, Russia

Glossary

biome – a large community of plants and animals suited for that place and climate.

coastline – the line where land meets water.

port – a place where ships load and unload, and its nearby town or city.

taiga – the strip of subarctic evergreen forest that covers much of the northern parts of North America, Europe, and Asia.

tundra – one of the huge plains in the arctic region of North America, Europe, and Asia. Trees do not grow on tundra.

Index

animals 16

Arctic Ocean 10

arts 20

Asia 4

Caucasus Mountains 8

climate 6

Europe 4

geography 6, 8, 10

Moscow 12

Mount Elbrus 8

Neva River 14

Pacific Ocean 10

plants 16, 18

population 12

Saint Petersburg 14

size 4, 6

Tolstoy, Leo 20

Visit **abdokids.com** to access crafts, games, videos, and more!

Use Abdo Kids code

CRK5540

or scan this QR code!